MY HERESIES

poems

ALINA STEFANESCU

SARABANDE BOOKS | LOUISVILLE, KY

Publisher's Cataloging-In-Publication Data
(Provided by Cassidy Cataloguing Services, Inc.).

Names: Stefanescu, Alina, author.
Title: My heresies : poems / Alina Stefanescu.
Description: First edition. | Louisville, KY : Sarabande Books, [2025]
Identifiers: ISBN: 978-1-956046-37-3 (paperback) | 978-1-956046-38-0 (ebook)
Subjects: LCSH: Romanian Americans--Poetry. | Families--Poetry. | Life--Poetry. | Women--Poetry. | Love--Poetry. | LCGFT: Poetry.
Classification: LCC: PS3619.T4458 M9 2025 | DDC: 811/.6--dc23

Cover by Sarah Flood-Baumann.
Interior design by Danika Isdahl.

Printed in USA.
This book is printed on acid-free paper.
Sarabande Books is a nonprofit literary organization.

The Kentucky Arts Council, the state arts agency, supports Sarabande Books with state tax dollars and federal funding from the National Endowment for the Arts.

This book is dedicated to my maternal grandmother, Alina, the namesake who died two months before I was born.

Alina Gancevici

CONTENTS

MY HERESIES

Byline, Be Sky

You meet the birds
on their terrain, the gray of

chimney swifts
sifted from clouds like feathered cinders.

The sky is smoking
his halftime blunts—

this you watch
from the roof

of Birmingham's tallest building,
dream the flight without

foresight, without
knowledge of falling.

It may be wind, warming
the names we are given.

It may be trapped inside
naturalized, this smoothed stone

you wanted, the motion
down your son's boot, driving

stacks of sustained D's
across pianos—

If tempo is wind when loosed
from the arms of

Rilke's terrible angels,
even holiness cannot be loyal

to the three within Thee.
Unstable tripod, you are

severaled, torn from
your mother's wild tongue—

it is the world
who keeps calling
wings wrong.

Once you raced through high grass
to greet his scarecrow, two hands

holding your skirt aloft. Once you knew
fear is how children learn flying,

and the scars left by cars
are your byline—

all the stars are ours,
tinny bye-lines.

So say it.

Lay your I
on the bough
                    of this moment—

      dear buildings,
       let me

            go

O sky,

make
me

            stop

I

There is something between us better than love: a complicity.
Marguerite Yourcenar, *Fires*

Tonight, as You Pace the Garden

I am eating raw violets.

I am curious about the possessing
in the having-been possessed.

I am present for the pastness,
grass bears

my back. That birdbath
sprawled on its side has
forsaken its purpose—

it has given the snails a steeple
that is churchless.

You say lazy daisy but I am all
languor, I am all lolling

which means recovering
from visual pin tucks,

like halftime is a noun between goalposts
for people who want things

but I am all cheering
is what we do
to shush the loud crowd

inside. I am possessing
the bittiest breaths
of your pacing.

And the snails?
They possess the steeple—
the snails have a path to the sky

My Father Explains Why They Left Me Behind When Defecting

in Hoa Nguyen's unrelated future tense

You are the same to me.
The baby in the photo you were, dark
curls we kissed before fleeing.
Your mom was pregnant with
the one she birthed in america.
Your eyes didn't match.
One was yellower.
And no leaves on the lindens then
we didn't know if we'd see you again.
We didn't know if we'd see you again
and know leaves on the lindens, then.
One was yellower.
Your eyes didn't match
the one she birthed in america.
Your mom was pregnant with
curls we kissed before fleeing.
The baby in the photo you were, dark
you are. The same to me.

The Home Is Six Hens Which Never Lay Eggs

The home is those animals
who eat and keep trying. Two parents,
a little sister, the trusted friendship
of crimson azaleas. The hearth

is your native tongue, heating
the porch; the horas who rise after
sunset, the fire-dances competing
with 100-foot magnolias for stature:

this standing above to look
downward. And the children
count sheep inside the concussion
of solid pink bricks. The house

bent, the house suave as plums
that hit the ground before ripening.
The home is those useless seeds
your mom snuck over an ocean

from Romania: one single tall plum,
the solitary survivor. The tree refused
to give fruit if left on a lawn, alone. The baby
shipped to grow through the drumbeat

of lawnmowers. The heart is the brick
of porch floor, the absent family, the dead
voices, gossiping between paper envelopes,
words abandoned near unopened doors.

Cosmologies

A partisan of erotic absolutism, reticent megalomaniac even among the divers, at the same time messenger of the halo, Paul Celan.

Paul Celan (in the first prose poem he signed as Paul Celan)

I

We began in cosmic obscenity—
the lascivious bang was the sound
of light's excess opening its mouth.

The first word wasn't love, was it?
It was this once that sat upon a time we can't locate
in physics. It was the science of bread
being broken and eaten.

I am still terrible at division.
I halved my whimpers when my mother vanished.
It is still easier to subtract than to be
split.

II

You said every lie is a nail in the eye of the dead.

My mother and I flit between French and Romanian
when sharing a bottle of wine. In hindsight, the past tense overrides
the presence.

My mother numbered her conquests but left them
nameless because sex is a comet that begins in a memory of longing.
The mother is the creature who teaches us to seduce it. "Sweetie,
you must do everything once," she says. "Refuse to repent,
and don't ever forget . . ."

She leaves the door open in ellipses so others may join us.
Simonides cringes, steps in. "From the bitter thyme I suck my verse,"
he says of the blooming not-yet. Svetlana Boym lights a Kent,
confirms: "One can estrange the common place but then
one has to estrange one's own estrangement."

Walter Benjamin plays with a twig. "Let no thought pass incognito,"
he says, "and keep your notebook as strictly as the authorities keep their
register of aliens." Ewa Lipska spills coffee on the tabletop just to
demonstrate, once and for all, that "the boundaries of the soul and
the boundaries of countries do not overlap."

Sonnet at the Ghost Commune

Paul Celan begins with an act of self-naming.
The poem claims the invention of self
on a Bucharest windowsill. Poets put

the moon in its place
at the horn of the table
on the shoe of the satyr folding laundry into bohemian ballet.

We lay a flowering dogwood in the foreground
to undress our ancestors on a train whose pain is a window.

In a hallway, the staccato of shoes
discovers parquet, the chic domestique
of loose aprons. I was eight

when Mom's linden first entered the room;
all attendant bold ghouls in my blood,
the disco of verso.

I Nominate the Kudzu to Keep Secrets

Someone patches a driveway.
Someone pours cement into the wound's open mouth.
It is Sunday's raw quietude, the screws in my knee burning,
the green behind the house keeping secrets. Mom's voice mixes
with wind chimes in this romanian summon, this private *ah-LEE-nah*
in which I am known. My name on her tongue is not
forked as in school, as in public, the UH-*lay*-NUH I'm made
by implication: Assimil Ate the intonation.
I cannot return as one daughter without giving up
this southern galaxy, the bible belt
bit in my mouth, the churning
breath of barred owls outside the house
I am fifteen forever, and not knowing better.

I Nominate the Linden to Continue Its Service as Tree of Longing and Aromatic Futility

for the boys of my youths

The battle between linden and kudzu
begins early. Those who know me
know lindens line the streets of my ink.
Summer looms every scent into raiment. I let this dress
me. So you knew where I had been that night in Bucharest
when the songs of street violins turned ruinous.
Maybe dimming matters. Maybe light is a
preexisting condition for love, an auspice of longing:
remembering your hands on this body in hospital bedding,
your belief pain might render me faithful.
I trust nocturnes, the arms of old trees, the verb
allegiance nestling close to *allegation*. Like the promise,
a pledge seeds its end in asphalt, concrete, there is no word for
the worthiness. I could not be. Cancel the stars.
Cancel the eyes yet glued to them.

Karaoke Duet for Eastern Bloc Defectors

Doru's Song	*Lydia's Song*
I've come to a land whose lindens	I've come to a land whose signs
hold no stories of the love between	refer to things acquired, purchased,
my ancestors—	rootless—
I've come to make metal	I've come to give birth to an american,
for spacecraft.	an anchor—I left
I brought my blue jeans.	the other baby behind
	but I brought my blue jeans.
I've come to be owned by no Party	
outside the animal	I've come because my mother died
of my own thoughts.	& my father won't wait forever
	before finding another story
I've come to unmurder my conscience and	to replace her.
make the parents who can't see me proud.	
I honor my ancestors by being the best	I pour love into *ciorba* to keep
metallurgist in my department.	from scaring my daughters
	who have grown in the local delusions
I've come for the grandchildren	of privacy, distance, rage—
born to freedom.	
	I hope my success will protect my children
I leave our house, our kin, the dignity	from the powerlessness of life without
of family history, the ease of a	family or kinship—
known tongue—	
	my love for these girls
I lose my community, my friends, my	so intense, so bereft of borders,
childhood, the homeland where I learned	no american word
the verb *love*. No word exists here	can marry it. And no
that can replace it.	man is god enough to carry it.

Childhood Confession for Zagajewski's "Illustrious Caesura"

The tree doesn't shudder before
lightning strikes it—not even the tallest pine sees that fire coming.

But I knew the unforgivable
thunder of watching boys
split each other's faces on asphalt, the steeple's shadow laid

over us all. The fathers of the sons
looked away in loving-splendor.

Each tree leaves limbs in the yardage.
Each shade protects a certain

uncertainty.

The commitment of my gaze—the painstaking
lineation of blood and cruelty—remains
inexcusable. Because I couldn't rejoin

the good world, I saved it
to ruin the page.

Socialization #2: Sky in the Other Language

Tell me about the time of the giants.

My father begins with its ending—in a flood

Those who get displaced by water lose their lineage. Purple medusas grow on the faces of children whose bodies remember surviving the waters. Your great-grandfather had a birthmark on his forehead that resembles the one on your thigh. As for the giants, they were gigantic—and generous. If a soul from Moldovan Hills needed a pot to make mămăligă, he took a step into a Hungarian neighbor's yard and filled it with water from Nine Seas. No one got angry. A giant could borrow trees from the Nine Forests to heat the pot, and procure kindling with ease from Bulgarian neighbors. A giant is three steps away from anything we humans can imagine. The giants knew no nation-states; their hearts were physically bigger than mountains. Their needs were gargantuan but had not yet found a form that demanded the destruction of others.

Then who am I?

My father laughs

He says the land of the giants
had no word for scarcity
no noun for absence &

no
individual
acts.

II

They say that sexuality can be dangerously Dionysian. Nowhere do we need order more than at any orgy. What is form, in any case, but a bumbershoot held up against the absence of all cloud?

William Gass, *On Being Blue*

On the Sidewalk, Something Winged It

Some thing wing
ed

left its blue shell
open like a burst-mark

Something hatched
from the cracks
without ending

And you have been
there

You have wished to remember
being an egg, being wombed

and unknown
yet beloved by parties
eager to guess
your hue

Gender, like genre,
still blurs thee

You can't keep the
packing intact

The Thou indiscrete
from its covering

You want entire
armor of an omelet

You want the unriven
ontology

Bear at Băneasa

The bear behind bars
at the zoo in Băneasa is a stranger
to beech trees.

You learn this by pressing your cheeks
against iron, to show him you will do
anything to speak to him—

to ask in whispers
if he remembers the mountains
of his youth, the stigma of early stars,
persuade him to describe

the burden of claws
rendered useless. Even as a child,
you knew what you had to do
to find answers. Study him.

Study the creature as he once
studied the twig's sudden motion,
in the land before cages,
in the republic of reading rustlings

for omens. You are a child at zoo;
and the world is a book
with a bear.

Seduce it. You waited for him
three nights with the village boys
near the sheep's carcass. One of them
had a gun. There is a zoo
named Revenge in the city.

But you were conceived
in the raspberry thickets of a Carpathian trail
in the era when the woods belonged

to bears. Watch him pace the
cell in Băneasa, his realm narrowed
by the appetites of children carrying ice cream
and shiny balloons.

The jubilant eyes of the child
at that moment before the string slips
from the fingers and the cry is swallowed
by the sky. Coax it close enough to write.

Poem for the Black Bird

after Matthew Zapruder

Today I wept with the kids as we drove
the dirt roads, grass greener than ever, I felt it
closed. The meadows smothered dozing cows in clover
and violet. A certain valence. It came so close
to something nameless. I needed the omnivorous
metaphor, a golden omen. I needed to touch
its extreme beak with my mind, to know
it existed. That afternoon decades ago
when my mom went to Wal-Mart, the red poppies
ran across her skirt, her eyes bluer than melting glaciers.
She emerged with a bag, no explanation. And I drove
us back to the house my dad won by divorcing.
I don't remember how night descended, whether feathered
or furred, no poem-bird could hold it. Mom went inside
first. I stood near the pine and lied to love, lied to its face. I felt it
closed. And there was Mom, in the window,
unwrapping her purchase. She set a chair near the socket,
plugged in her pen. I watched her blaze the pine-panel walls
with a wood-burner. It wound round the rim of the room
and grew rounder, the part I didn't see coming.
You will never forget me, Doru. No one else left
their homeland for you. Her hands shook, pressing
words into the flesh of our home. The life she was
leaving. Her notes, that winding charred necklace,
encircling us. The bird was not black.
It was the color of fire absent smoke.
Please help me forget what it spoke.

Ode to Something Elusive

Not ozymandias or love this
morning, I could walk to the edge

of craving and never quit looking.
I followed piety along the tracks,

smoked a butt, measured the city's contingence,
slid two honeysuckles between my lips

in lieu of mints. The coal train
chuggled past in gold and black,

its slowness militant as
the lie a man offers his mistress,

harbinger of diamond
to come. I came
closest.

The sky suckled its coal-teat.
I did not know where I was,

what time wanted—
an epic. Tagged in red

beneath the bridge:
Dante wuz.

The Kraków Nude

The framed photo used to hang in the hall
of my single-mom apartment—hair loose, lips bit by laughter,
flesh naked but for a man's white cotton undies,
arms angled like unmapped pyramids behind my head.
In my apartment, the crushed velvet of black mold lined
each air vent. Valiant rats scattered their marble feces
across the floor. I read them like runes or coffee grounds
back then when the man I'd marry was merely a friend who
came over, drank whiskey, watched me blend baby food.
Back when the man was just a hot dude talking smack to my toddler,
acting shocked by the Kraków nude I kept hanging
on the wall near my room. I keep thinking
it was hot and I am not sorry, and now is the opposite of
then—when it was summer and I was younger
than freedom in eastern europe. It was decadent
and I was the owner of two tender breasts that rose
to toast the moment like swollen wine goblets.
I was pregnant and plotting how to escape the unwanted
parts I was not-yet: the abortion, then the intentional
miscarriage. Proudly, I wore the plenitude of my divine
crimes across my chest. I touched them as knights caress
silver armor, each fingertip remembering the emptied
casings which missed me—the torment of inches,
the rapture of millimeters, empyrean insolence.

Dear B—, would that you hadn't unlatched the symbols

When Thom Gunn admired
the hummingbirds giving blow jobs,
he did so in a letter to a friend.

Gunn didn't drag their slim beaks
into the room of the poem where beards
and ears judge our exposed orifices.

I am over. Are we closer
now. I am assuming you know
of the pink whale I painted
on the cover of our shared notebook.

It needed marking.
It needed me to leave

the wee words and stroam
the alleys between vacant warehouses,
to heed the birdsong of idling trucks.

I think everything is beaked
if you let me approach it

in verbs. I wrote three
words on my wrist: alone,

alone, alone. Behind the
assembled dumpsters,
the cold hunch of green mettle

and the hundred-studded dandelions
raising their yellow pricks
to cover the meadow in eyelets.

Mysterium, as Engraved on Pope's Tiara until the Reformation[1]

a gender-modified golden shovel involving Revelation 17:5

And so it begins to end. There—past the chair—
upon the floored mattress, his hands searched
her hair for wind. His eyes scoured her
forehead for omens. One scar in the left corner
was the stained window. Glass has its hued diction,
a color to clip silence's virtue. He needs a conjurable
name to pin to the lyre, to blame for the lure, a specificity
written in neap tides, a tower of saltine crackers.
Mystery dies when read closely. But he invents anyway:
Babylon, the brided lyric, groomed to expiate
the sex in the bar bathroom, against the wall, the
great suspicion that he was less cunning. And she knew
the surrounding tower of his scorn. Would he compare her to his
mother? Another mattress? A facsimile breast in the flesh
of grown mirrors? Night shelters its writhing
harlots with eyes like accidental sharps (mine among them)
and still, we refuse to accept how the instrument contrives
abominations, the scythed music
of our predicates. First there was
the irresistible honeyed mouth—the whole
earth was shaped to hold it.

[1] Until the time of Reformation, the Pope's tiara had the Mysterium engraved on it. The letters of the Mysterium were said to make up the number 666 ("Mother of harlots and abominations of the earth").

Evil Eye

the one which
began the
division
of labors,
the first
miracle—
an angel
who tumbles
can turn
into a
serpent
who trolls the garden
of your delights
but I was
your favorite—
she said
as she
toppled
from the
sky—O,
how she
fell for
envying
Adam,
that
monster
made in
God's
image,
the apple
of His
fickle
lil' eye

Light Does This Exposing

You want me to see you
as I see the written subject.

You resent the instability of being
seen in a light you judge
undeserving of love.

It is your lumière—
your bulb exposing the room
where I nurse a small mammal
who hasn't learned
dividing words
                    yet

                    from   shadows.

A fiction may be surveillance
technology. This is how
one begins an apologetics to kin—
the notion of self,
indistinguishable from
its audience.

I watch you so closely
love is my favorite invention.
A boat of close attentions
lying sideways.

Little Things: A Ring

Virtue is complicated. I mean
Catherine of Siena had her cake and got ate
by it. This is what happens to saints
when they marry tripartite entities.

One third gave her an invisible ring
crafted from his foreskin.
Another third denied it.
The third third kept quiet.

I, too, would appreciate
being courted at the leveling
of the sacred.

If I can't partake of the trifecta,
I will settle for that flaming
thing in the angel's right hand.

Look at you, Man, guarding
the Idea of a garden!

Look at all the swords and rings and lords
you forged to keep
Adam and Eve from returning.

Sonnet When Called Away from Ghost Commune by Howls

In the desert stars grew stadiums.
Boulders hedged my body like boyfriends
once mounted. I sat atop Bobby & Jimbo & Tim.
This thing I wanted from not seeing—to moisten
what deserts us, to overcome what devours by
desiccating the world. But Night kept silent.
The wolf's thirst chiseled the canyon range,
shaping routes for water to run. It was his
pain that laid canyons between hardness
& softening. The sun wins everything
the sky cannot tame. I follow the wild
that hunts me. We circle each other
like horses at opposite ends of a carousel,
my daughter's first constellations.

III

For what the hurrying eye has seen merely from the car it cannot retain, and the vanishing landscape leaves no more traces behind than it bears upon itself.
Theodor Adorno, *Minima Moralia*

Let no thought pass incognito, and keep your notebook as strictly as the authorities keep their register of aliens.
Walter Benjamin, "Writer's Technique in Thirteen Theses"

Infinitive Neo-Theology

For we cometh to judge the light paling the door, not the dark hall it obscures.
C. D. Wright

To run our tongues over the suns which divide us.

To savor the shape of a moment entering the mind by altering its relation to silence.

To hear him sing the Fall whole in the shower.

To wonder why only unborn angels are spared from touching the tainted ground.

To understand what binds the pitch to the oar or sound.

To find the avian in craving another creature completely.

To sight the demon in wanting to divine him.

To exist, as ruined by rapture, as buried in chords.

To claw the crypt in the opening door.

Even the Air is Violet Between Us

The clock ticks clematis.

Time is the sum of thinking one
could train voices to climb

                                        the same tendril.

Vines loom the awning
above.

The week passes in streaks   of odium
the fake aroma

of fresh laundry crawls in
through our windows
then stumbles out drunk
from neighboring dryers

                                        to stroll the streets.

Nothing stays quiet
or private.

Even the air serves his
memorandum to the tedium;
snails lineate the steps
like prayer beads.

Time is being detergent
to this estrangement
from thinking

                                        I could speak.

I'm not afraid of the heedless
plunge forward.
It is not that.

It is the flower's relation   to the vine.

It is the windless apostrophe.
one doesn't expect

I wear the blue dress
when met with no scruples

It is the tremble
when touching
                the covering.

your eyes remove

yet need.

On the Emotional Life of Angels

You quoted a learned man
when you said baptism was the metaphysical button: the Big Beep
that alerts one's guardian angel to start guarding.

Do we each have our own?
Or do we share guardians like toddlers at daycare?

I suspect officials keep us tethered to nowhere
and birthlands. My guard is notoriously hard to understand;
he mutters like balkans crossing

the borders of language, crossing in me
has no stable shore. The angels born in eastern europe
must be many-tongued polylinguists.

They wear diacritic stains on their foreheads.
May I am one. Maybe I am two. Maybe I am a sausage.
Maybe I am a stew. Maybe I'm an unreliable

narrator for western tourists who like
a clean narrative arc. You quoted the Big Beep.
I told you I can't speak

when my guard jiggles the key and his eye fills the cell
with aeviternal glee, the terminal joy of having a front seat
to divine radiance.

Local Left-Behindlings are stocking guns and 3D
printers for the apocalyptic festivities. They told our son
that the devil who destroys everything will be romanian.

I am guarding my angel for him.

Apostrophe on Natural Numbers

The whole season is a triptych of tailgates.
I wade the shallows, doze the news, admire the light
dudes contrive to brutalize others, the bardo of headless
statues on screens, the monster one was

before being chosen, before being named part of the 144,000,
the natural number which brackets the saved. A certain quantity
is redeemed *a priori*. You cite the source as revelation
book 7, verse 4—and mention *sealant*.

We watch joggers circle the pond but your silence
never discloses who is sealed and who is damned to leak
out the last days in a kitschy lake house. Suddenly, three clouds
vanish like eggs who've been raptured by raptors.

The hot keeps growing hotter. I read the books
you know by heart. Between the sixth seal and the seventh,
I dream of making love to Jacques Ellul, dragging my
deranged hair across his chest like a bookmark.

Spondeo, per Social Media

I guarantee to render a like sum
on your profile, that social equal
which appears in the pantisocracy of your fond disinterest.

Logomancy is romantic when paired with rum.
Logomancy is red as delirium on the vine.

I swear by the same hand
which cannot decide

whether to maunder or manustuprate tonight
all the penumbrae seem sprung

Indictment for Failure to Conjugate

Failure to absorb the verb
and modify the actor accordingly.

To sit and
play dumb.

Because I could not promise symbiosis,
I was generous with respite, easy to conquest,
wound taut as a jet's final flight deck.

Because I could not submerge myself
entirely, I let them drown me in bits, in inches,
in frantic up-and-downers—Enough

to know
how it felt

Enough to claim *I'm all yours*
for the breathless duration of disappearance.

Because I did not want to owe
them, I rented: I let them
own me. The poem combs
her hair for the cliff.

Me, to the Poem—at the Warehouse

with Marina Tsvetaeva, Osip Mandelstam, and Lena Constante

Climb the hill of each other
staying hungry. You must

sew your
eyes open for this.

Candlelight makes it seem as if the hand goes
numb before the throat.

You are dream's color technician,
warning the night who was me before bleach.

The opposite of ecstasy
is automation. I feel something
has passed, something has

shifted in the darkness
like loose dentures.

Dead verbs lather my scalp
like a church who must service
the male host first.

Climb the hill of each hunger
like a show trial. Your head

is the stake
and the

shakedown.

I Nominate the Magnolia as Sexiest Tree

Forget the stories of fairy-tailed monsters
that spooked you: the wolves in southern
ladies' eyes will eat you for brunch
with ambrosia salad. There is no forest outside
the tradition's silk tent: an alien must wed
a southern man to keep the south in her mouth
from losing the ballpark. I wear a skirt to seem
worthy of wind lifting it skyward. I practice
kissing the trunk's shoulder. I plant a tiny
magnolia in the middle of my middle
daughter's name so none can deny
her placement.

Why One Cloud is Kin to Not Liking

The reason my husband's family doesn't like me is that I am loud and talkative and elitist. I am a know-it-all book nerd who acts certain about all the outrageous horseshit galloping out of her horsetooth-mouth. These are the facts.

The park is emptied by a pandemic and everything is warm, cozy, abandoned until one single cloud creeps over the sun and reveals the power of chilling. Go away, my son commands the cloud. I, who'd never dare address a cloud like this, can still admire the mammal that is loud and talkative and elitist in his presumptive relations with condensation events.

The truth about clouds is that they haven't happened:

They are collections of things which may come to pass or change the sun's frame on a landscape. It rained the whole day of our November wedding, like a Guns N' Roses song, and the sun came out in time for the sunset. We married for its orangeade eyes. *They never liked me.* Even then in my white handsewn dress, I was presumptuous. My bare feet were a form of private aggression against middle-class values. In their eyes, I could only be baggage, the single mother he saved. The cloud will move eventually, I tell my son. The cloud cannot be the reason everything is ruined, I tell his family. The park is empty.

Housemaid's Knee

I am getting a housemaid's knee, kneeling here gulping beauty.
Apocryphal Amelia Earhart

This is the knee's response
to the poem. It is the callous
that can't afford a white dress,

the price of innocence rising
like oceans over retiring houses.
And day, itself—a constellation

waiting for bed. You must
write dread, the uncle of confusion,
the second cousin of curses.

Only water matters for the
mornings woken drunk.
You must explain how obedience

poemed you, and left holes
in the wall with its studmarks.

What you want is not
    the virgin's posture,
not the pedestal's connivance
with power. You want the secret
of the machine at midnight.

The First Carcass is a Marital Milestone

Four carcasses, actually—
feathers strewn across the grass
like post-party streamers.

We suspect a fox
in the end of the hens.

A neighbor defines a fox as *fur*
that resembles a skinny dog
but moves like a Slinky.

We have no one to blame
but ourselves, I tell the man
as he shovels the remains
into a hole behind our house.

The children collect feathers
and tape them to their shirts.

They wear our failure
like ghosts who know nothing
can protect them.

The man wishes I wasn't
so sensitive: death is just
part of life. That night,

we study the animal
kingdom and I am
bewildered by the brutal

geometry. There is
a pyramid with our
folks on top.

Self-Portrait with Flower Crown Woven from Allergenic Weeds

The cause (etiology) and course of development (pathogenesis) of a disease are not congruent: in the case of numerous diseases, we know why they came into being without knowing what the cause is.

László Földényi, *Melancholy*

I skim the near-saints: the Italian whose
indigestion improved after being struck by lightning,
the Sardinian nun who bound her own tongue
with an iron ring and then hung from the ceiling
shaped like a cross. Some women lean in

too far.

We married without a car.
Some humans

believe

the stem signifies
the flower's
origin.

Make Me That Way

with fragments of a line from a lullaby by Neko Case

A dark diction in the depths of these deeds that have made me. The comb administers the hand. I plaited my hair & wrote your name on my wrist with his pen. Old verbs candled me pewter, or plated for man. Phrase me the way you like most.

*

Make me what they say
an angel
          is to be
alembicated into the human viscera.

Make me
the cherub
          they say
is actually
          the storm winds

which carry god in gold clouds
when he decides
                    to visit
          the impulse of his creations.

Make me
the thunder
          you meet
near the bier,
               smitten with fear

   of being found
    as sound

Pavane for Fools

Near the cost of knowing lies the sin
of being known.

I think you love me the way a barstool
indulges the loose matchstick, the way a skyline buries
its blue in gold sequins, the way you sighed when I dragged
my left shoe across the amp to pretend
you were something
like music.

There is poison in this scenario.
There are chemicals in the creek accruing
cancer as we sleep—and the death
already in us, grinding her teeth.

The cost of knowing the poems I've abandoned
is excruciation—the words lost, the screwed
sensation of limitations hardening to frost. I think
you love me like beauty loves terror in Rilke's troth.

The poem teaches six peacocks to dance but lacks
nouns to bear the heft of what is loomed in the name
of convenience. The weft adjusts by widening its step.
Evil eyes stack their indictments against us.

Poem in the Key of C-Sharp Minor

The lover is a tree.

And I lay beneath
him—the sodden world
wet as the mouth of the man who delivers
the planet's first commencement address,

the beginning that binds
voices to one another, knotting
    words.

    A We, said He.   *—but there were others.*

Adam lifted his alto to meet the
divine, and varied his tone six times
to cover the utterings of all known angels.

There is little to see
in the key of haunted cliché.
An eon of words. And you do not
speak as I scale him.

Say nothing as I skin knees
to ascend the throats of the dying,
the winged

        angle I was
before reaching the peak.
The geometry of turning away, the fall
                calling.

                The score
        watching from the half-paved
        driveway as I lose my goodness
        in yours.

All day, it rains inside us—

Two Years After Our Dog, Pinka, Got Hit by a Car on Halloween and Died Before Our Eyes as the Kids Howled in Ghost Costumes on the Front Lawn

We babysit two guinea pigs named Bitch and Luther.
You dream Pinka went on tour with Metallica. I can't

look at October grass without gagging. Someone
retrace our grins to give back the night I dressed up

as Emma Goldman. What line did we cross in letting her in?
When someone says puppies, Max cringes. Milla hopes

dogs have a heaven without cars and humans. Micah knows
love is only here for a minute before the giddy retirees

run it over. An arpeggio scalds the throat. I was ten
when the bully confessed an old man hurt him. Suffering

begs the question of cruelty, or which egg hatched first.
One makes a nest to draw robins closer. We house-sit

three hens. The kids learn to swim. We coddle a school
of pet spiders. We keep a bowl stocked with vociferous rocks

and bogged marvels. A window opens upon the poem's accident:
you say each costumed creature must find shiny words

to placate their beast. We tell ourselves plants talk. I cannot.

"An Intense Sense of Victimization"

We must secure the existence of our people and a future for white children.[2]
David Lane's "14 words" slogan for US neo-Nazi movement

An intense sense of victimization is common among white nationalists.

I read that male porcupines hop about on one leg with a paw
draped over raw genitals after coitus.

Shame is common in Catholic families. A *closet drama*
is meant to be read aloud rather than performed.

Quantum entanglement complicates the ashes during cremation.

One may ultimate-frisbee his way through an ozone warning.

A spider flies by electrostatic repulsion, making use of negative
electromagnetic charges in the air. See *unwinged*.

LockerRoomTalk is a popular neo-Nazi podcast.

The *Rise Above Movement* started in California. The men discovered their affinities
at a gym amid the aroma of wet iron: a nagging desire to see Trump go further.

These RAMs were "not racist." They were *proud* of their *heritage*;
they identified as *warriors* for the right to white skin supremacy.

Two founding RAMs were active duty Marines.

A *bildungsroman* may include a timeline of the protagonist's early life.

An intense sense of victimization is common among Trump voters.

I have read that Proust wrote in bed, stretched on one side, for hours at a time.

I'm writing in bed, stretched on one side like Proust when he decided
writing was the only partner he wanted.

Look: the wrist falls asleep before the elbow.

Plants share a *negative* charge with the ground. They grow up and out and into positively charged air.

The juxtaposition of unlike things causes invisible electric fields to form around plant branches & leaves like secret patches of *positivity*.

One may Pizzagate with the wind in his hair or the sun in his bootstraps.

An intense sense of victimization is common among *religious fundamentalists*.

Locker-room talk is where they grow up and come out manly.

"God has a place for each person," Dzhokhar Tsarnaev wrote on the side of the canoe, using his own blood for ink.

The orphans of silence gather in the orchard to collect fallen plums.

Eyes like tasers bring a twitch to the face.

A *bildungsroman* may include the persistence of garlic.

Shame is common when suffering is bondage.

God is the most intense eagle.

The whole field at stake.

[2] Italicized words and quotations were taken from various news articles on the rise of the neo-fascist Right.

After Reading the Extended Family Hate Mail

Let's walk away from the rotting dung-heaps, their diameters
seeking verbs in our mouths, the ice cream truck hollering
the same hollow requiem as wooden flowerbeds hold out
their reds like tulip-pimps in the park of Good Fridays.

Forgive the hatred of blood's relation. Don't hold me against
the shallow delights of small mammals with blue balloons,
or the dog running his nose over the arched back of the squirrel's doom,
those corneas frozen open, my eyes frozen like this in you—*everything*
is a word for an ocean. An ocean is a puddle if we kneel closer.

heretic / relapse / apostate / idolator

On May 30, 1431, Joan of Arc recanted her confession pursuant to a visit by an angel. As a result of her recantation, Joan was taken to the funeral pyre wearing a paper crown reading: "Heretic. Relapse. Apostate. Idolator." Her ashes were thrown into the Seine.

We make love, detangle limbs. Somewhere on earth men plot their apocalypse. Humans crave an epiphenomenal hit. You say wanting an end is not the same as seeking a future. You believe things begin and then go on *forever*, which is a word for *not yet*. You say sincerity is purely aesthetic preference. Your favorite god is Hermes, deity of thieves and cunning, maestro of eloquence, inventor of lyre, flute, alphabet, human sacrifice, and the technique of making fire by twirling a stick. I know the opposite of heresy is belief.

Revelation 18:24

a golden shovel with gender adjustments—for a shadow on a sidewalk

And the loose ends
in me could barely look at you flinchless.
It felt like borrowed brightness. Or
was it the rapture's tightness? My way of being
found is not without pleasure:
the whir of the email opening, the
blood of a bitten lip, the studious dance
of attentiveness . . . to grasp your intent.
Prophets have meant things forever,
and who can mean blazes so fervently? Which undertone
of text fails to inflame its iterations? Hagiographies need
saints as deeds need kisses, as pews need knees
and kneelings. Should I defy ritual to be new to you? To be
of novel heresy? The snakebite recites its secret:
all harmless skin is worth tasting. Would
that you knew me. Would that you
were some truer thing. Would that the
slain parts of humans greened into vines
upon a brick wall and you could walk
the city's entirety tonight. Would that the unrelenting
earth wasn't the book I kept misreading.

Loose Exegesis

a gender-modified golden shovel of Revelations 17:6

And how the pros sparkled! I thought I'd play this game best
when playing my betters. Up close to the net, pivotless,
I felt myself most alive when being slaughtered. Everyone
saw the shame, how swiftly it came to its descendant. Dark heirs
then cookies in a star tin. I licked the sweetness from each surface.
I thought I could handle it, friend. Maybe a tinge even
wondered. But you read me like a feather set on fire is the entirety
with us—flame between two pages sharing a bench. Your words or Scriabin's.
Great Coincidence, please take what you've won. Conceive my
admiration. Your head in my words—eros, cinders.

Medea's Apostrophe in Storm

I wanted an uninhabited island
but you make *light* of me.

You do what Scriabin did to the sea.

You make *merry* to score
what you adore.

The infamous savior said of his mortal enemy:
Behold, I see Satan falling from heaven
like lightning. Lucifer was the first winged
thing to fall.

Your angel started it all.

You make light to ignore the thunder's roar.

You overlook that he had been light before.

Each You makes it harder to die without hurting someone.

The last letter was an acrostic envoi.

IV

Something that has really occurred, that's what death is.
Everything else is not something that has occurred.
It's not even something that is occurring.
It's a belly button, the shadow of a leaf, it's a skid on the surface.
Alexander Vvedensky (translated by Eugene Ostashevsky)

On the Death of the Day of the Bear

with Candlemas in Transylvania,
for my mother—and César Vallejo

I will die on the day of the bear, when frost
loosens its lips from lindens—on the day the bear
leaves winter's den to taste the world's unnumbing.

People will say she seeks the sun out of love
for her own shadow: the vow of spring in running
water. The bear will pause to sip from a stream;

after this first drink, the bear is most dangerous.
She is wild, they will say of my mother after she flees
the homeland. She has died, they will mutter upon finding

her tattered bear coat, the one she wore over an ocean
to prepare for American winters. Thus the groundhog
will gain ground, mark its new time in our minds.

And she who died in the shadow of bears
will rise in the suburbs, the streetlights, the pines.

Posthumous Journey IV

On the day my thigh-stitch purples,
I discover a rusted pitchfork in a new tale.
The auspiciousness is an infection, a failure
to dissolve without fever. And I remember
the times people knew of my surgeries.
I remember the humiliating publicity
of almost dying and then being tired
of comforting others who almost lost me
for their near-losings. It was like being in Kraków
in the early 2000s again, and miscarrying
a thing alone. I could barely tell a soul.
I am alive. It hurts so much. It is extraordinary.

“And we really didn’t know”

A contrapuntal karaoke tune for eastern bloc children, titled after a line by Ryszard Krynicki

we didn’t know you   were children before you
were parents and   believed airports
were spaces   between events
so horas were trails   toward circles
we couldn’t imagine   how much you packed into
silence   the one leather suitcase
we failed to decipher   the lies behind extra consonants
walls padded by accents   we helped you plant tulips
in wood garden beds   and sow kisses, nostalgia-buds,
and you were still   children each time a seed fell
in the soil’s little scoop   the hole in the flag you
believed something   could grow from
the exilic credo   and we really didn’t exist
at least not   like the dead
like the absent   persisted and lived
we could not be   that rich
in your mouths   remembering

Socialization #7: American Playground Game for Kids

I goes to the slide
And claims it
for others

Mine appears

the animals with large bows
planted atop their heads by diligent mothers
coalesce into giggles

We is here

I who is not
permitted
to enter the We
lies to an Us
by standing above such constructs

standing alone at the top
of the slide
like a headless bow
I becomes You
who knows It

Socialization # 12: American Playground Game for Parents

They sits on the bench
watching small animals gather sticks
and rocks and pebbles

We doesn't think
He would actually
do It but

I near the tree
imagines the
one wants to tell We

They might
They just may
They can do anything

when the ambulance arrives
in shiny red lights and rhinestones
They break into pieces

of My goodness

“Every problem cries in its own language”

title taken from Tomas Tranströmer’s “Our History” (translated by Robin Fulton)

I

The dinner with slender candles.
A daughter too anxious to sit. Toboggans
in her belly track the blizzard outside.
Ice on the eaves. Her fear of conflict. I explain it
to my father in Romanian to keep from shaming her.
She hates attention—the substance snow lays
over quiet bushes, pinned by landscapes they can’t escape.
Child like a naked wick who knows fire, she is
twelve, or two hundred raw surfaces altered by angles of light.
My husband pours water over ice, its crackle
the snapping of fingers, the warning I should stop speaking
in that foreign language, to keep others from feeling
left out. My throat like the narrowest inch of a vase.
At the table. His hand near the ice, the vise.

II

When Homer says the Sirens
offer us omniscience, all I think is
They are noisy. And the hospital parking deck is packed
for the weekend no one planned.

No one wants to be disoriented by pending diagnoses
with price tags. To know everything

is to be petrified, stunned to stone,
incapable of motion, a statue in the plaza
perpetually shat upon by pigeons, the lovers cheating
on each other near your immobile toes.

And silence is witness
doing nothing—like the leafless
tree in Mom's yard who asks too much of the sky,
expecting its image in it.

III

The first time I read Robert Musil, I was nursing
an infant near the fungus-degraded dogwood
and all I could see was his wife, buried by vintage fridge magnets,
counterpoint to the life a man could live—and write.
To be decades of dinner. A cravat and a pitcher.
The presence of yam pies and casseroles.
The conditional's guest list. Her mother
tongue banished from table
like a bitch worth no bone.
Like a she-dog offered this
singular silence to lick,
this hardened un-
known, to crouch
in the shadows,
disowned.

I Wove a Wildflower Crown of Kinned Dreads for You

We walk by faith, not by sight, and have knowledge in mirrors and riddles.
Maximus the Confessor, as quoted in letter from poet's mother

No stallion, no salve, no savior,
I tell the cloud near my foot
on the sidewalk
before burying forked tongues in the hair
beneath my hoodie
to race shadows with children.

My kinned dreads, my kindreds: the end of any
extended family. It is easier to disappear than be
the reason for scarcity.

I love the loosening of dandelion fluff in the meadow
regardless. I walk the kids home
and return to the metaphysics of emptiness
alone. I curl near a train track
to draw the moon closer.
Near the woodpile, I spot two coyotes;
it is rare to glimpse a pair.
And John says *it is fulfilled* when he means
fulfillment is occurring, inconceivably.

If the riddle finds my mother, tell her
grief is the glutton of all
I am glut

Leaflostness

I believe a leaf of grass is no less than the journey-work of the stars.
Walt Whitman

To satchel the words
to carry the loss of you
across an ocean.

O bleak motion,
I read motes filtered through
dust, the gild of your laughter.

A shaken blue lamp covets
the peace of small beasts who still need

the nest of
me. One voice freezes

the other keeps moving,
weakening music.

Weakening music
the other keeps moving
me. One voices freezes

the nest of
the peace of small beasts who still need.

A shaken blue lamp covets
dust, the gild of your laughter.

I read motes filtered through
oblique motion

across an ocean:
to carry the loss of you,
to satchel the words.

V

(FILMING THE SKY)

At what point is an ending ruined by our anticipation of it? I mean, the sky was unimaginable cirrus that week in December of 1989. Clouds cleared for the Dictator's final speech. His televised face broadcast from the balcony, electrified by platitudes. No one believed. The booing spread over the crowd like fake plastic leaves. Sidewalks smothered with screams. As police began beating families, state cameramen followed orders to *film the sky*—

> the documentary record of the romanian
> "revolution" includes these
> images of transposed
>
> *cloudlessness*—

In Case Sanda Ungureanu Comes Over

On the patio, a fresh pinafore of crepe myrtle
crumbling. I tell the puddle to return to the cloud.
I sweep the gray cement steps we can't incant into
the arms of elms. In this balance where looking back tastes blasphemous,
there is a Bucharest bar where my father courts Sanda Ungureanu,
who is not yet the love of Ion P. Coulianu's life, not yet the wake
of his flight to Chicago. Coulianu's unsolved murder lies in wait.
Yes, romanians have a thing for Fate—the dictatorship of secrets
spills like ashes from blacklisted urns as we smudge ancestral soot
on our foreheads. We know each other by anonymous ash prints.
We find ourselves in dark fingermarks we can't forget.
Our minds divine the brains of secret police.

Are your fingers stained black with these silences?
Meet me in the exile of an Alabama twilight
amid the tea-scape of forbidden lindens,
behind the raw silk of Patsy Cline karaoked in a slavic
accent. Again, Bunicu declaims the star's broken heart.
Time, here, is measured by one hundred lines of poetry
crawling the walls of the room. We trust the star to keep dying
forever. We trust the eyes to hide crying with laughter.

There is a knife to mirror self on the edge of this
terror. But the blade feels like love, I tell my partner.

> Give me a nude shoulder, the least
> perfect breast to cut these milk teeth.
>
> Give me rotten plums, sheepskin drums,
> a fist of garlic flower blooming
> from a grave that *keeps*
> *its bones home.*

Viaticum

We pay to arrive, alive. After we
die, a meretricious person who loved us
may lay the viaticum atop the tongue
attached to our carcass. My grandfather
said if I talked too much, I would croak
with my mouth cracked open. Blessed
be the bed-head who gets buried as their
12:00 a.m. self, for they will inherit
the most festive ferrying. My mother
laid her palm on my bladebone and
said: *Don't look for the nodus.* She eyed
the suitcase I'd packed for romania—
added three cartons of Kents, two
*Playboy*s, a lipstick kiss. I left my family
in the States to go it alone over borders.
One half of me is all-american currency,
the other half would trade anything to keep
moving. In the homeland, the exchange on the train
occurred without introduction, without explanation.
The officials said nothing as they accepted
the lurid fare. Blessed be the mother
who knows her daughter's nightmares
will fruit. The summer of my
eloquent degradation began with a barter,
a small bet. The world is the casino.
If one knows the tell, it is a curse
to name it—a *blestem* to acknowledge
the exchange which comes with the payment.
Dear romania, land of my fucked mythomania,
why do your men take eternity with them?
I go back to visit the dead. I pay my respects
in the country where hidden taxes haunt
the train hallways, where bodies are zombied
by language, by *habar n-am*, by habit.

The Dictator's Secret Censors

Comrade Bone, why are you doing such pessimistic work?
Securitate official to artist Rudolf Bone, September 1989

You've written about everything
except celery, my man said, just after I'd finished
titling "The Celery Sagas"—

Later that night, I asked him
to read it. He demanded to know
if I was joking—

There is no such thing as coincidence,
my mom used to say, whenever she spoke
to her father in Romania—

Whenever she asked about
his heart or his health, and the line went
dead, it sounded busy.

A Little like Kierkegaard

for things buried at the foot of the flowering

Dear man, my will is worthless.

I mean my absence is the reason
you love me. And you love to
hate me, a little. Like your

intense one, I am disgusted
by mystic tokens and emblems
of amorous convention.

This is why I saved all my letters
from X's and planted them
in the rosewood dresser
made from a linden.

The First Gust of Special Relativity Is Weightlessness

Did it begin

when Einstein watched men wash the windows
of very tall buildings

and imagined how falling felt?

The theorist borrows a silhouette's terror
to build his edifice.

The sun is a man with big hands
on the couch

and the sky is his

origin. There is no duo
to local velocity, no duet.

I write to you
from the Icarus
in each of us, from the word

for existing
between aboveness
and asphalt.

I mean light on the pillow hisses when bussed
by a fan blade.

I mean fog is how clouds tongue
the ground.

The losing comes later, a night with no
windows, the stained cup of
lightspeed

you left on the floor,
all energy and mass, interchangeable—

Did it begin when
the sun became a man

abandoning the idea
of distance

in a bed? The specificity of
sex with insignificant others

has its masochistic
nocturne.

I write from
the sadist's
secret fretwork.

I have fallen
to know

how falling felt
and nothing sprung from it.

I have measured acceleration
in altering tempo,

the speed at which time expands
when you leave me

relatively speaking
there is nothing

worth keeping
for nothing—

The Street's Poorest Spirit Is a Poem with Too Many Images

One neighbor owns seven guns of great value.
Her blue plaster virgin stares me down
over the stone birdbath. Valor grooms
atrocity into statues. Guilt glues me to place
like the anklet one hides to keep from losing.
I roam the porch, eye on the known, beholden,
head like a bucket of foam. Hark! Here comes the aposiopesis—
the gods argue among Himselves.

Étude in Blue Minor

A cloud survives for ten minutes
on average, before dissolving
into someone's blue eyes, or the
edge of a scorpion's
sighs.

It is a complex
violence—the poem
memory devises from waiting
to become rain—the syntax
of expectation
needling the brain, the bravado
of cars parked like classical
guitars in paved places—
Did I *compose*
them?

As a teen, I notched
the wood above my bed.
Each line staked a claim.
Each spike marked a
a book in my head
a dream
I had
read—

and I am
still scoring
forgiveness—this
labor of returning
to the perilous world
the words one has
needed most
from it.

Postcard with Scene Near the River Where Virginia Woolf Drowned

I dreamt I was competing for her heart on the trail which led to the river. The green geometry of shade, of space, of light—a sense of being nowhere and yet bound to an immense vacuum. The treadmill of wild grass, the trail of others who went this way before me. Like you, god comes to me in the wrong language so the man thinks I want roses. The singularity accompanies me to the shore where tearing occurs. Time has no margin for error. Today is today until there is no tomorrow. We are born to be torn by ontology, the postcards of shorelines. A young boy parks his paper boat in the eye's margin. It is easier to err than to ask forgiveness, he says. The river riots through my head like the unwritten. Love is folly. I am laudanum. Water circles my ankles like iron scarves. Nouns leave their shoes near the larkspur. As if seeking Mandelstam's republic is my worst weakness. As if swimming is the ending of life rather than the beginning of wetness. As if writing is always a doormat and never an ardor for sky.

We Keep Driving

for Maggie Smith

You can't sleep, your head wired
by sirens. All those fears sound the same up close—
every edge shares its sluiced thunder, every nightmare
wears its loose cotton nightie.

You wake up soaked in it.
The kids want sausage casserole,
a dish rich as the ad you've rehearsed—
this motherhood, this late capitalist magic, this recipe
for being perfectly good.

You fail the bake-test. Slit the cereal
box open, pour it over a migraine, rouse the cock-a-hoop
voice you rent to make aimlessness sound exciting.
You don't know where you're going but there are wheels
in the Turkish coffee and the echoes of last night's tornadoes
mangle the road. You point out the rolled
azalea buds—the things waiting to open. You feel
old. The teen son clears his throat
to say geese have teeth on their tongues
            which they use to eat souls.

You believe it. Bits of blown-off roofs look up
from the ditches. The youngest counts colts
in the meadows, dreams of riding
a palomino.

            Mothers know
the cereal box you opened keeps one
from thinking about the box that stays closed.

Hell, you love these kids more than
mayo on french fries, more than raspberry mousse at midnight,
more than your own mother swore she loved you.

This is the algebra of ashes—
the truest things stay impossible
to prove. The youngest raises two

hands to show she is
so many fingers. She says
her mind wants to *grow* but

her heart wants to ride
its own saddle—her heart would rather
steal the horse she imagines
than own

the horse it is
sold.

Other Horses

My child's invisible horse returns differently, daily,
the way a favorite dress reshapes the flesh with each carving.
Marvel is the little one who dreams the body permits it.
Exuberance is the idiotic azaleas, the encore of their
annual resplendence. No romance in Romeo & Juliet,
no eternity and no respite in family hatred. Requiems
aside, those who romanticize being locked outside kinship
lack experience, or they lie.[3] Other horses, other gardens.
Tonight the oak trunk is furious at what the boy
knived into it. The vow is leaden. The owl abandons
her ascending sequence. And sadness is the lens
who kins the wound's strangeness.

[3] Stupid pyre. Wretched soap opera. Brutal portraiture.
Craven allure in fondling agony and imagining a solution
from the Pottery Barn soul on your self-affirming sofa.

Sky B-Sides

O pink linen apron, kinned to failure,
walls & wails share monochrome at midnight.

In the closet, each punctuation
marks the silence where horror catches its sniveling breath.

O monotone, bust me open like beer pong
in basements

I was sober
I was left frontal lobe
encephalomalacia

who kept her
self secret. Tell the son
love is soil, grass the gesture.

Tell the grrrls to save their
brains, screw their hymens.

O Head-in-the-Clouds, name the last
cake you baked from scratch
now call yourself
mommy.

A friend offers her magic ritual to help
bury grief but you cannot
buy it.

Not even for free will
you accept the lilied closure.

Go on—fuck the sky
like a backseat B-side
for nothing

is for nothing—
tag His walls
with red paint
when sheep sleep.

Parousia for My Children

The best time
to get lost is
when a cloud
dissolves on
your forehead.
The best friend
is a berserker
who lines your
nostrils with
detritus

—each layer adds warmth to waiting

What comes
first eventually
curves when
clouds rain.
Grass is the
spine you must
lay in to buy
time to try
harder. I
have lied
to you for
so many
years it
feels like
a book

—each layer adds weight to ending

Do not
flinch when
the inter-
rogations
commence.
Is it the
shame who
indicts the
shameless?

In an Elevator with Ashbery, Crossing Stanzas Bashfully

This poem is not concerned with language.

Not concerned with clauses or splendor's intended awning.

Not tracking the dissolute significance in the presence of that slurred cologne.

Not intrigued by the scent's attachments, the perfume's tailed fusillade.

Could not care less about connecting the odor of him to a corner in the crowded
room.

Could barely care less about which is stranger: the one who exists or the one who
remembers.

This poem is not interested in naming the nameless.

Not aiming to rekindle ferocity.

Not pining for that erotic velocity.

Not hiding the one who keeps moving behind his word.

Dream for Christina

Breathe on me still, star, sister.
Randall Jarrell, "The Meteorite"

I am standing beside you in Voronca's target-shooting shack
dressed as a seagull. You are folding a notebook page into
an octagonal shape and shaking your head. A wind demon
presses hair into our mouths and I am a hybrid who is trying
to explain that I flew over an ocean and massacred innocent
birds to stand inside the forest you wrote in stolen feathers
because I can't trust anyone else to translate me
into myself. Am I stranger in person
as a bird dream?
There is a shattered
eggshell near your sandal. There is a life that broke
open before it could be chosen. There is more tenderness
than one can fathom in wearing what never happened.
The wing I swallowed believes our bones have eons
to say to each other, and bracelets to knot, yet.

Alternative Index Discovered in Franz Kafka's Notebooks

All of this is a continuation of the lie, but . . . if I remain consistent, it comes close to the truth.

Franz Kafka

i "I'm supposed to serve as a nude model for a Saint Sebastian": Ibid., 186.
i "emotionally impossible, for how could one even": Ibid., 317.
i "have a little toy hammer in place of a heart": Ibid., 323.

ii "look at the floor": Ibid., 334.
ii "its neckline is filled with tulle": Ibid., 370.

iii "am sad that a shirt is pinching my neck, am damned": Ibid., 335.
iii "decaying and falling over": Ibid., 319.
iii "The Virgins etc.": Ibid., 132.
iii "bound to a tree until they turn blue": Ibid., 367.
iii "everything can be risked": Ibid., 240.
iii "on a beautiful horse": Ibid., 262.
iii "this is": Ibid., 256.
iii "not nearly so great as the lament led one to believe": Ibid., 373.

iv "The torment": Ibid., 169.
iv "covered with filth and slime": Ibid., 257.
iv "prolonged, inexorable dissatisfaction": Ibid., 223.
iv "Long torment." Ibid., 224.
iv "all the torment": Ibid., 233.
iv "because she lifted her skirts like this and like this and like this": Ibid., 239.

v "This is how it is in all bedrooms." Ibid., 389.
v "her hands through her hair": Ibid., 346.
v "illuminated by the gaslight": Ibid., 120.
v "this filth": Ibid., 382.
v "dripping with": Ibid., 382.
v "this wretched little happiness": Ibid., 389.
v "this burden": Ibid., 382.
v "this clenching": Ibid., 256.
v "this contempt": Ibid., 385.

vi “Each has only the experience that his affliction grants”: Ibid., 281.
vi “but I’m afraid to write about it”: Ibid., 217.

viii “I in my craving”: Ibid., 391.
viii “to arouse historical interest”: Ibid., 161.
viii “patent leather boots”: Ibid., 213.
viii “the girl’s voice in the choir”: Ibid., 376.
viii “a little ball”: Ibid., 217.
viii “blown up”: Ibid., 399.
viii “like little fires”: Ibid., 195.
viii “doing needlework”: Ibid., 420.

ix “Strauss’ ‘Frühlingsstimmen’”: Ibid., 596.
ix “Short fainting spell”: Ibid., 194.
ix “a paw close to my face”: Ibid., 149.
ix “silhouette of”: Ibid., 324.
ix “an unshakeable judgment”: Ibid., 226.
ix “seen with small binoculars”: Ibid., 568.
ix “rainless and still”: Ibid., 421.

x “I have lost myself to F.”: Ibid., 263.
x “The window was open”: Ibid., 282.
x “the moonlight fell through”: Ibid., 343.
x “the skylight”: Ibid., 343.
x “almost”: Ibid., 343.
x “Herder’s wife”: Ibid., 210.

xi “a baby is crying”: Ibid., 355.
xi “I stand there with my evil eye”: Ibid., 286.
xi “like a bagpipe”: Ibid., 408.
xi “growing muddled”: Ibid., 313.
xi “I”: Ibid., 482.
xi “ruin”: Ibid., 371.
xi “everything that doesn’t relate to literature”: Ibid., 298.

xii “Nothing else can ever satisfy me.” Ibid., 286.
xii “but the onslaught”: Ibid., 298.
xii “the all-too-great”: Ibid., 129.

xii "inner need for it": Ibid., 291.
xii "two as I am": Ibid., 134.
xii "Today I got Kierkegaard": Ibid., 303.

xiii "I mounted my horse and sat down firmly in the saddle." Ibid., 353.
xiii "all the signs of dilettantism": Ibid., 444.
xiii "aberrations with girls despite all headaches": Ibid., 416.
xiii "always the same": Ibid., 440.
xiii "rat hole of wretched ulterior": Ibid., 382.
xiii "marriage or Berlin": Ibid., 263.
xiii "This feeling of falseness I have when writing": Ibid., 168.
xiii "burned by it": Ibid., 194.

xiv "L. confessed his gonorrhea to me": Ibid., 47.
xiv "maliciously": Ibid., 323.
xiv "trembling like a sick animal": Ibid., 275.
xiv "in light of": Ibid, 326.
xiv "ulterior motives": Ibid., 382.
xiv "a band of little golden beads around a tanned neck": Ibid., 296.
xiv "The other view: saved for later": Ibid., 473.
xiv "dirty, oldish, complete stranger with wrinkled thighs": Ibid., 489.
xiv "irretrievably abandoned": Ibid., 326.
xiv "The third view: already forgotten": Ibid., 473.

xv "hovering somewhere in emptiness": Ibid., 313.
xv "the inkwell": Ibid., 313.

xviii "table music": Ibid., 348.
xviii "she is again the center of it all": Ibid., 358.
xviii "torn pants": Ibid., 349.
xviii "tribunal in the hotel": Ibid., 347.
xviii "asphalt like the apparatus": Ibid., 504.
xviii "three times": Ibid., 234.
xviii "to ruin": Ibid., 393.
xviii "lamps in the asphalt as in a river": Ibid., 504.

xix "exciting statues of saints on the Karlsbruecke": Ibid., 417.
xix "The invention of the devil." Ibid., 223.

xix “in a corner”: Ibid., 313.

xix “to run one little finger over one’s eyebrows”: Ibid., 194.

xix “as with a furiously torn-open tin can.” Ibid., 307.

xix “striving”: Ibid., p. 159.

xx “I am lost”: Ibid., 348.

xx “I can’t chase the stories through the nights”: Ibid., 377.

xx “I can no longer go on writing.” Ibid., 370.

xx “I am turning into stone”: Ibid., 348.

xx “in bed”: Ibid., 267.

xx “I make ghosts for myself”: Ibid., 208.

xx “on the toilet”: Ibid., 411.

xx “I have finally made F. unhappy”: Ibid., 371.

xx “I am completely alone”: Ibid., 355.

xx “a moment I thought”: Ibid., 208.

xx “when I woke up”: Ibid., 343.

xx “I saw something real in the description of the landscape”: Ibid., 208.

Letter with Heirloom "Pen"

for Lydia, with pen running

Like snails during drought, the daughters
curl into catastrophic shells on the couch

they say they know
I'll croak in my sleep

like you did. One hundred percent I'll keel over
dead in some hotel bed across an ocean, a distance so intense
no starwish could stop me.

—And your ghost unfolds its grin
as I bend over to tickle the mortified mollusks,

as I anoint their foreheads with laughter:
Nothing like that can ever happen

I assure them. I giggle, I parry, I joust. Darkness
descends. The snails wander to bed.

Now I am the room's single animal:
the monster who opens the shoebox
to lift the crumbling lipstick

to feel closer to you
is to drag the horrid pink hue

over my frown. *Currente calamo*, now
you are with me. You exist

in this posthumous clown
who creeps into her daughters' bathroom
to scribble a message across the mirror.

We two use the same Lancôme pen,
the same shade, the identical:

I love you!
See you soon, scumpi!

We end with the same smear of lips
as a signature. I kiss the mirror

like a virgin and ask the last
words to last forever.

Skies melt the blue of glaciers.

This is a trick one plays with horizons,
I tell your ghost. You taught me
the worst is coming; the unbelievable

is near. We must abandon our daughters
with lies left on mirrors

between all the air
and the oceans,
there is this *love,*

Mom.

Socialization #23: Family Art Museum Visit

Another pietà. A French queen. A Hollywood staple
by Annie Leibovitz. A princess in velvet adorned on a chaise.
A widow weeping. A glamorous starlet. Another queen.

In the art museum, a mind is an envelope.
Each painting falls in. A child is the image's first
communicant. We read the captions to ourselves.

When men speak of the unborn angels,
I suspect an immaculate flesh bore them
privately. Everything private is mistaken for

preciousness. A hernia hidden beneath a corset.
All beings are bourne by a laboring body. Life is art's
spite. The womb that gets used finds no respite.

Extraordinary Premises

I saw an angel in a teacup on a screen.
The Invisible Hand slaughtered it.

Demand evolved to give us inner tubes and blue eyes.
Fireworks libate the billboard behind our house. Relentlessly, the markets provide
magic. We overheard *many die quietly*, and felt like commercials

for hearths lit by fake logs. The faux-hissing
of screens puzzled me. The extraordinary premises
the ordinary. I wore my palm

like an eye patch to silence the migraine, and stood
near the rotting wood window like a screened seraphim,
a girl on film making pain precious.

I pimped my pain-peonies for social media.
Later, a wise screen told me that starlings take turns
sitting on eggs, though the mom always nominates
herself for the night shift.

The surgeon said do not run, do not bend, do not move
except to get water or go potty. *If you can't follow instructions, no one*
can help you. A screen told me two cute
radiologists read my film wrong.

I wore a fake log to the wake for my third
misdiagnosis. We overheard an eye patch telling a teacup
demand had evolved into a mother-like figure.
My stitches kept getting infected. My peonies
acquired some fungi. A screen sold me

a pain angel of positivity.
Only death and this little stool for company.
I stayed lit for the starlings on night shifts.

Epistle for the Man Standing on the Beach Before Everything Ends

My grandmother kept a cock in the shed
to announce the morning of her own annunciation.
She knew the end was built into

the song. But the taste of tire squalls
are singed to my tongue; I can't decipher
where we begin outside attachment.

I can't sift a melody from what you said
that midnight decades ago when I took off my clothes
and ran into the ocean whose moon

painted me platinum, whose hands plaited
my hair for my grandmother's cenotaph.
Oh P, I am still empty, still queered

by the scent of wet stone, still hiding
behind reckless laughter and braggadocio
for the rodeo of our arguments,

for the fears swarming the cul-de-sac of
a streetlamp, and the light keeping us
bound to its threshold.

The gate is still there
and still missing. I can't decipher
an end to the mystery.

Portrait of Couple at Fifteenth Anniversary

On our fifteenth anniversary, with the assistance of fireflies,
I cut your hair in an abandoned cemetery. The surround sound

of dusklit red dirt is our family tradition. We invented
each other from fragments of flotsam and landfills.

For each trim, the kids chose which grave to honor,
which names to detain as sound. Our hair is loud and

lives all over the land. I maintain the map of our offerings
in the glove box—a malediction, protective talisman

against the elegant viciousness of american dreams
and southern idioms. When they blessed our little ole hearts,

they damned them to hell. There is this curse of southern gospel
between the ochre sunset and the guns under their windshields.

Yours is the face of the lover for whom I live in prison.
I am the umpire of weeping for insects scattered by midnight

and the amp of quiet kids hiding in corners with invisible friends.
Daylight is the frenzied tumbler who approaches the emptiness

of each emotion untended, each lollipop unwrapped.
Thunder is the instant before lightning strikes the sky's

bass note: All swallows know this. The stars are
the taste of love. The vow is the unbidden anklet

of algae. I want to meet to the big alto whose moon
is our Oreo pie. I want him to watch

the metonymy, the missing, the thing about the streetlamps
in history. The heresy the stars are when you touch me.

Epiphaneia

Dear six winged
many-I'd
things

I have been

done by

bright offerings and trios of kings.
I have been offered free van rides
in return for a blow job.

I have been blessed,
boggled, bowled over by the lushness
of strangers and violins.

When the blackbird
shatters its head
against the window near our bed,

when the flight fumbles,
falters, stalls —
and the winged thing

is dead,

I shall

be quiet

as a triumvirate.

O void
I have   been

the bird, the paned glass
the grass
bearing the fallen
carcass.

We decimate
our selves
when aiming to see
the thing   beyond
the thing

we have   been

done by —

love,
is it —
the brightness

Acknowledgments

With gratitude to the poets, writers, editors, and friends whose words and lives are stitched on the underside of my eyelids, and whose kindness has been a bridge at a time when the ground beneath this body crumbled. With additional gratitude to Major Jackson for sharing "In an Elevator with Ashbery, Crossing Stanzas Bashfully" on his wonderful podcast, *The Slowdown*, and to the generous humans and diligent hands behind the following journals in which these poems were first published:

8 Poems: "After Reading the Extended Family Hate Mail"
Apofenie: "Me, to the Poem—at the Warehouse"
American Poetry Review: "Medea's Apostrophe in Storm"
Ballast: "Mysterium, as Engraved on Pope's Tiara until the Reformation"
Blood Tree Literature: "On the Sidewalk, Something Winged It"
Boats Against the Current: "The First Gust of Special Relativity Is Weightlessness"
Border Crossings: "Light Does This Exposing"
Brooklyn Rail: "Alternative Index Discovered in Franz Kafka's Notebooks""
Cagibi: "In Case Sanda Ungureanu Comes Over"
Cincinnati Review miCRo: "Why One Cloud Is Kin to Not Liking"
Copihue Poetry: "Viaticum," "Extraordinary Premises"
Copper Nickel: "On the Death of the Day of the Bear"
Counterclock: "My Father Explains Why They Left Me Behind When Defecting," "Sonnet When Called Away from Ghost Commune by Howls"
Couplet Poetry: "I Nominate the Linden to Continue Its Service as Tree of Longing and Aromatic Futility," "I Nominate the Magnolia as Sexiest Tree"
Dishsoap Quarterly: "The Kraków Nude"
Five South: "The Home Is Six Hens Which Never Lay Eggs"
Hoosac Institute: "Dear B—, would that you hadn't unlatched the symbols"
Ilanot Review: "Socialization #2: Sky in the Other Language"
Kenyon Review: "Byline, Be Sky," "Ode to Something Elusive"
Moist Poetry Journal: "We Keep Driving"
New World Writing Quarterly: "Housemaid's Knee"
Poet Lore: "Indictment for Failure to Conjugate"
Poetry: "Poem for the Black Bird"
Salamander: "Two Years After Our Dog, Pinka, Got Hit by a Car on Halloween and Died Before Our Eyes as the Kids Howled in Ghost Costumes on the Front Lawn"

Spoon River Poetry Review: “And we really didn’t know,” “Even the Air is Violet Between Us,” “Leaflostness”

Notes on the Poems

The prefatory epigraph comes from Marguerite Yourcenar's book *Fires*, a personal reworking of various ancient hagiographies—a book whose subversions influence my own. / Paul Celan's first signed poem comes from Petre Solomon's memoir of their friendship. / Several poems draw on superstitions surrounding "evil eyes," or envy, in Romanian culture. Angels with many eyes are dangerous. Of course "the green ice" of hell for women involves marriage, and the envy that arises in families. Perhaps it speaks in dialogue with Psalm 40, where we are told that burnt-offering and sin-offering are no longer required. Only praise and supplication. Certainly, it refers to Isaiah 49, verses 1 and 2: "He made my mouth like a sharp sword."/ The poem "Make Me That Way" plays on a fragment—"wrapped in the depths of these deeds that have made me"—found in Neko Case's song "Furnace Room Lullaby." / Several poems draw on the various theological explanations for Satan's fall from heaven, or for the first sin—which may have been that of an angel. "Medea's Apostrophe in Storm" outlines Origen's theory. "Evil Eye" is based on Justin the Martyr's theory. / In the poem titled "Extraordinary Premises" the line "Only death and this little stool for company" comes from Andrew Davis's translation of Osip Mandelstam's *Voronezh Notebooks.* / The "posthumous journey" poem follows the mode created by Polish poet Ryszard Krynicki. / Some of the earlier poems in this book were inspired by Romanian mythology about the origins of the stars, some of which was found in a book on my mother's shelves, titled *Mitologia Românească.* / "All this is a continuation of the lie, but . . . if I remain consistent, it comes close to the truth": I retained all of Kafka's capitalizations and punctuations in the excerpted fragments. The same is true for the quotations of Ross Benjamin's endnotes. Source: Franz Kafka, *The Diaries of Franz Kafka*, translated by Ross Benjamin (Schocken Books, 2023). / Photo of Alina Gancevici taken by Gheorge Gancevici.

Alina Stefanescu was born in Romania and lives in Birmingham, Alabama, with her partner and several intense mammals. Recent books include a creative nonfiction chapbook, *Ribald* (Bull City Press Inch Series, 2020), and *Dor*, which won the Wandering Aengus Book Award (Wandering Aengus Press, 2021). Her debut fiction collection, *Every Mask I Tried On*, won the Brighthorse Books Prize (2018). Alina's poems, essays, and fiction can be found in *Prairie Schooner*, *North American Review*, *World Literature Today*, *Pleiades*, *Poetry*, *BOMB*, *Crab Creek Review*, and others. She serves as editor, reviewer, and critic for various journals and is currently working on a novel-like creature. More online at www.alinastefanescuwriter.com.

photo credit: Him

Sarabande Books is a nonprofit independent literary press headquartered in Louisville, Kentucky. Established in 1994 to champion poetry, fiction, and essay, we are committed to creating lasting editions that honor exceptional writing. With over two hundred titles in print, we have earned a dedicated readership and a national reputation as a publisher of diverse forms and innovative voices.